POETIC PRAISES

Poetic Praises

Overcoming addiction with praise

Written By
KIMEISHA D. COX

Jai Publishing House Incorporated
Atlanta, GA • www.jaipublishing.com

Copyright © 2020 by Kimeisha D. Cox

All rights reserved. No part of this publication may be reproduced, distributed, or transmitted in any form or by any means, including photocopying, recording, or other electronic or mechanical methods, without the prior written permission of the publisher. For permission requests, write to the publisher, addressed "Attention: Permissions Coordinator," at the address below.

Jai Publishing House Incorporated
1230 Peachtree Street NE, 19th Floor
Atlanta, Georgia 30309
www.jaipublishing.com

Ordering Information: Quantity sales. Special discounts are available on quantity purchases by corporations, associations, and others. For details, contact the publisher at the address above.

Scripture quotations taken from the
Holy Bible, King James Version.

The Publisher is not responsible for websites (or their content) that are not owned by the publisher. The views expressed in this publication are those of the authors and do not necessarily reflect the official policy or position of any other agency, organization, employer or company associated with the publisher.

Printed in the United States of America

ISBN: 978-1-7366613-9-0

Dedication

I dedicated this book to my family

Chapbook
Table of Contents

Preface 9

The Birth of Jahawa 15

Set Free 21

He Made Me Whole Again 25

Agape Grace 31

Mercy, Faith and Righteousness 35

The Potter's Hand 41

A Reason For the Season 45

Blessing From Above 51

Compassion 57

A Love Like Yours 65

Grace, Blessings and Glory 73

My Lord 79

Fighting To Live 83

Amen 89

Catch It, Check It, Change It 93

Unsolicted Memories 99

About the Author 105

Acknowledgments 107

Preface

This is the first of several books that I will be writing as a new author. Some of my poems may sound similar in many ways, but as you read on you will understand the different perspectives of reflections that I am writing about.

To being delivered from a 20-year crack addiction, how I was able to find forgiveness and peace in my broken heart after being abandoned by someone who was supposed to love and protect me, being completely healed from Leukemia at the age of 13, to being diagnosed with Stage 3 Metastatic Estrogen positive Breast Cancer at the age of 44.

I grew up in church attending church on a regular (sometimes daily) basis, and was an avid member of the choir. But as I grew older, I started straying away from Church and God, heading down some paths of life that have made me the STRONG WOMAN I am today!

I have ALWAYS had a passion for writing, even at times just scribbling words and drawing whatever my imagination came up with.

Back then I couldn't understand why writing was so important to me, but I never gave up and today I still have a passion for writing.

Never in my wildest imagination would I have believed that God would use me to write about and share with others how I was able to overcome and endure so many obstacles in my life.

It may not always feel good or things don't go as you had planned... JUST TRUST GOD and His ALL knowing Omnipotence.

Try seeing things from His perspective; pray for patience (which a lot of us don't have) sit still, be quiet and watch God show up and show out.

Stay woke and be aware because He may just be protecting you from yourself, something or someone trying to harm you.

"You will face many defeats in life, but never let yourself be defeated."

— Maya Angelou

For whatsoever is born of God overcometh the world: and this is the victory that overcometh the world, even our faith.

Photo by Chris Lawton on Unsplash

The birth of Jahawa

"For I know the thoughts that I think toward you, saith the Lord, thoughts of peace, and not of evil, to give you an expected end."

Jeremiah 29:11

Lord Jesus, heal.
Heal in me whatever You see needs healing.
Heal me of whatever might separate me from You.
Heal my memory, heal my heart, heal my emotions,
heal my spirit, heal my body, heal my soul.
Lay Your hands gently upon me and Heal me through Your love for me.
AMEN.

This poem was birthed on October 3, 2020 at 7:03 a.m. after having another inspiring spirit stirring phone call from my publishing consultant.

We talked about all walks of life which gives me a chance of knowing her as more than just my publishing consultant, and gives me the opportunity to share a little more about myself.

I feel this spiritual connection when talking with her that I haven't felt in quite some time. I guess that is because she makes you feel confident, comfortable & so secure enough to want to open up and talk about anything.

What I appreciate most about her is how open, honest and soft spoken, but straight to the point she is. She says that I inspire her with my poetry. SHE INSPIRES ME THE MOST EACH TIME WE TALK, TEXT, OR EMAIL EACH OTHER WHEN SHE UPDATES ME ON THE PROGRESS OF MY BOOK, OR JUST TO HAVE A GENERAL CONVERSATION.

Yahawa could not have chosen a better publishing company to help me get my book published and out to the community. I want to thank you ladies Jai Publishing House (you know who you are) and everyone else who works behind the scene to make my dream of getting my book published......YOU ALL ROCK!!!

Yahawa

Yahawa's will is always perfect and always on time, I am referring to when He pushed back the launching of my book's time line.

Yahawa is definitely not finished with me yet, on a daily basis He puts my Faith to the test.

Yahawa continues to mold me creating my life for the better, it started in 2013 when I was Baptized while living in a homeless shelter.

Yahawa always has a Ram in the bush when it seems like I am down to nothing, He shows up and shows out providing my needs with an overflow of blessings.

"Who is this Yahawa" I speak about some may say? He is my Lord, my Father, my Savior Who guides me through this unknown path of life day after day.

Set Free

> "I can do all things through Christ
> which strengtheneth me."
>
> Philippians 4:13

In this written work, I am giving all praises to The Most High for setting me free from the crippling & deadly clutches of a drug-induced life that I lived for many years.

When I became addicted to the drug called 'crack cocaine', my son was still in Elementary School.

When I was finally tired of being sick and tired, I surrendered my life back to Christ allowing Him to do what I had failed to do on my own several times before my baby Michael was grown and in his 20's.

I missed out on so many memories and milestones with him and had to get to know my son all over again..... but this time as a man.

Set Free

Hallelujah, Amen I have been set free, from the grips of the enemy that tried to kill me.

What a joyous feeling it is to know that you are one of God's chosen, when your heart fills with hope again after your Spirit has been quenched and broken.

He Made Me Whole Again

> Jesus answered, "Verily, verily, I say unto thee, Except a man be born of water and of the Spirit, he cannot enter into the kingdom of God."
>
> John 3:5

This poem was inspired after being baptized on June 2, 2013 at the age of 42. I finally understood the true meaning of what it meant and why it was so important for me to become a new creature in Christ.

I referred myself to the Prodigal (Daughter) Son ready to return home to the Father. There were things that I had not repented, or forgiven myself for holding on to so many regrets from my past.

I could not shake them loose on my own and I knew the only way to begin to heal Spiritually and Mentally was to turn my life back over to Christ.

He Made Me Whole Again

It's me, it's me. I'm finally free and have been turned around so graciously.

This poem I write comes from the heart, I have been reconnected to the Father I have been set apart.

God has blessed me in abundance in so many ways I am found in His favor day after day.

I praise Him continuously from the time I awake, for His love and mercy and everlasting grace.

I've been cleansed and delivered by the potters hands, He continues to restore my soul giving me chance after chance.

He has made whole again when I was broken, I am grateful to know that I am one of His chosen.

Agape Grace

> "8 For by grace are ye saved through faith; and that not of yourselves: it is the gift of God: 9 Not of works, lest any man should boast."
>
> Ephesians 2:8-9

"AGAPE" is the highest form of love, charity of love God for man and of man for God.

"GRACE" means the free and unmerited favor of God.

This poem was inspired by the combining of such amazing words.

Agape Grace

Agape grace that's what it is, because of His love we are able to live.

He looks beyond our sins and faults when we don't obey the way we were taught.

He guides us down the path of life to keep our feet from trouble and strife.

He strengthens us when we are weak which teaches us to be strong and meek.

We don't deserve the love He gives, but AGAPE GRACE is our Father's will.

Mercy, Faith and Righteousness

> "That your faith should not stand in the wisdom of men, but in the power of God."
>
> 1 Corinthians 2:5

Trust your faith, not your struggle.

The storm will end.

Let it build you, not break you.

Mercy, Faith and Righteousness

Thank You Father for favoring me to see another day, for the many blessings of Mercy You give at times when I go astray.

You delivered me from the darkness and brought me into the light, You calmed my oh so VENGEFUL heart when it was filled with spite.

Hold on to the little faith being the size of a mustard seed, I struggled and strived to hold deep within every word in the Bible I read.

I thirst for righteousness day and night for the gift of living water, while worshipping You on bending knees as I bow before the altar.

With every poem I write You allows me to tell a story, You blessed me with the gift of writing and I gratefully give you Glory.

"Success is to be measured not so much by the position that one has reached in life as by the obstacles which he has overcome."

— Booker T. Washington

The Potter's Hand

> "But now, O Lord, thou art our father; we are the clay, and thou our potter; and we all are the work of thy hand."
>
> Isaiah 64:8

I have been broken so many times and I know I was only strengthen by the POTTER'S HAND. Every time He would reshape and mold me.

Each time He would add a little more knowledge, grace, wisdom and strength to get to the next level.

I know now that He allows us to be broken so He can add a little more of Himself, and remove more of us.

The Potter's Hand

God knew my name before I was formed and cradled me in His loving arms.

Breathing life through my nostrils He enabled me to live, filled with the knowledge, grace and wisdom He abundantly gives.

I was created solely from the rib of a man, woven together oh so gently with the touch of His hands.

Heed my word when I say to you that God is truly real, when I was stricken with Cancer He whispered to me.....Daughter you are healed.

A Reason For the Season

"To every thing there is a season, and a time to every purpose under the heaven..."

Ecclesiastes 3:1

The mind is a powerful force.

It can enslave us or empower us.

It can plunge us into the depths of misery or take us to the heights of ecstasy.

Learn to use the power wisely.

When I wrote this poem, I was going through a whirlwind of an emotional rollercoaster. It is a no brainer for me to speak the words of encouragement over the lives of others in need, but it was a dreadful task finding the strength or words to encourage myself that night.

It felt like the world was on my shoulders and my mind was filled with clutter of negativity when searching for something to help me through my crisis.

My depression had such an overwhelming stronghold on me that I decided to post it on my Facebook social media page. My page was suddenly filled with support, love, prayers and understanding.

The decision to share my crisis was because there are others who still suffer from and living silently with some form of mental emotional imbalance, too ashamed or fearful to ask for help.

The world has labeled people like us as MENTALLY ILL, which in society is deemed as a misfit, crazy or insane and is also responsible for many others not getting the proper help they need.

But on this night, the support was so overwhelming others were no longer afraid to admit that they were living with the same mental emotional imbalance as I was.

The breakthrough for me that night was I realized the reason I was spiritually led to share my pain wasn't for me........ God was using me to reach those still suffering in silence to let them know that they are alone.

To "everything there is a season" emphasizes that all emotions and actions, both negative and positive, have important meaning and people should experience them all throughout life. (Biblical Commentary)

A Reason For The Season

Thank You Father for holding me close and always hearing my prayers, at times when I feel so distant from You by letting me know You are near.

For family and friends I call upon when I'm feeling all alone, to share encouraging words of wisdom to help me through my storms.

I find myself supporting others saying Everything happens for a reason, but when the tables are turned and I can't find the words they remind me....

IT'S ONLY FOR A SEASON!

Blessing From Above

> "But seek ye first the kingdom of God, and his righteousness; and all these things shall be added unto you."
>
> Matthew 6:33

The young lady in this poem I am referring to was a center sister of mine named, Paris.

In 2012, both of us were residents at Atlanta Mission Women & Children Homeless Shelter a Faith-based facility.

We began talking about the poems I had displayed in the halls on the community boards, and I explained to her that in the future I wanted to one day create a book and publish my poems.

She then asked me if I had ever thought about putting my poems on clothing, such as the onesies that babies wear. She suggested that idea being that babies get so much attention, and if my poems were on their clothing, my work would get some attention too.

At that moment I felt that it was a message from Above, it was the Holy Spirit using her to guide me in the direction to become prosperously successful in my future plans.

God will use anyone and anything to convey a message to us. All we must do is humble ourselves, pray for discernment, be willing to have an open mind, accept His plan, and let His will be done in our lives.

Blessing From Above

I met a young lady who inspired me, suggesting the value of my poems beyond what I could see.

She gave me ideas I never thought about, they were blessings from God without a doubt.

They were full of hope.

What she said today, is how to promote my poems another way.

The suggestion she gave me was simple you see, it was to have them printed on little baby onesies.

Compassion

"Let all your things be done with charity."

1 Corinthians 16:14

"For thou, Lord, art good, and ready to forgive; and plenteous in mercy unto all them that call upon thee."

Psalm 86:5

All of my written works were Spirit-lead by an event that took place in my life at some point and time.

I was inspired to write most of them when I resided at the Atlanta Missions in their Personal Development Program (PDP).

The PDP was created and designed to heal those seeking mental and spiritual restoration, enabling you to sit still long enough for God to begin the healing process in whatever area of your life that was needed (your mind, heart, soul and spirit).

They housed women from all walks of life and from all parts of the world seeking help.

Divine intervention led me to that particular Program to begin my healing process and restore my relationship with Christ.

If it had not been for the Lord, "LORD OH LORD WHERE WOULD I BE?"

Compassion

You have been there with me through every
stumble and fall, regardless of what the day
may bring it's Your name I always call.

When I am feeling weak with my heart heavy
and my head hung down, You give me the

strength I seek with meekness and grace
sending praises towards the clouds.

I place my trouble at your feet because
You care for me, I wait to hear the voice of
reasoning as I am on bending knees.

Thank You Lord for loving me with a graceful
heart of compassion, for showing me that

humbling grace regardless of my actions.

Everyone can say "I Love You" but not everyone really means it. So, believe it when you feel it, not when you hear it.

Author Unknown

A Love Like Yours

> "Whoso findeth a wife findeth a good thing, and obtaineth favour of the Lord."
>
> Proverbs 18:22

I Met the one whom God chose for me to be with, and not me choosing him against God's will. I finally realized that no matter how bad you want something or someone, if it is not in God's will and plan for your life, it is not going to happen.

Almost 2 years later, we are still standing as our friendship and companionship grows stronger each day. I can admit that we have had some storms, mountains and valleys that we faced, but God said, "Two are stronger together than one," as we have passed every test that came before us by the grace of God.

When times were tough, we were not sure if we were going to make it. As we stood the test of time, we realized we are where we needed to be and that is with each other.

I thank God for bringing him in my life at a time I felt lost, unloved and alone. Bit by bit, he was able to chip away at the wall I erected; forcing me to relinquish the over-guardedness, permitting the ability to let him love, care for, understand, provide and protect me the way God intended it to be.

A Love Like Yours

A love like yours I thought I would never find, the moment you said Hello I knew you would be mine.

You tried to deny your attraction and wanted to run away, not knowing that I had permeated your heart you decided to stay.

We have so much in common it seems hard to believe, it's like a star lit sky filled with a light cool breeze.

God blessed me with you and I will do my best, to show you my strength and compassion when we face our trials and tests.

You are one of the loves of my

life and this I want you to know, I pray our bond gets stronger and more compatible as our relationship continues to grow.

Grace, Blessings and Glory

> "If the Son therefore shall make you free, ye shall be free indeed."
>
> John 8:36

> "For as he thinketh in his heart, so is he: Eat and drink, saith he to thee; but his heart is not with thee."
>
> Proverbs 23:7

This is the very first poem I was SPIRITUALLY led to write a few months after being delivered from the stronghold of a crack cocaine.

When I heard others say, "Once an addict always an addict", I REFUSED TO SPEAK THAT OVER MY LIFE.

Words have POWER and you MUST be careful what you speak over, in and through your life as well as the lives of others. I was not going to keep referring to myself as an addict, because I knew that I had been delivered, set free and made whole again once and for all.

This was my commitment to God that I would not return to that life of misery, shame, hurt, regret, disgusting, loathing and lack of self-respect that He freed me from.

THIS POEM CAN ALSO BE USED AS AN AFFIRMATION & PRAYER OF COMMITMENT

Grace, Blessings and Glory

I give to you my God above praying 365 with a heart full of love.

I call on You every day of the year, because I need You Lord to keep me near.

I lean on You to see me through and answer my prayers as to what I should do.

You give me grace and a peace of mind, without you Lord I don't think I could find.

The glory and blessings You have given me; without You, I don't know where I would be.

For a long , long time I felt

disgraced, then my Lord and Saviour Jesus put glory before my face.

Without God in my life He can break me down and all my sins I confess will not be found.

I made a promise to God which is a fact, I have given Him my life and I won't take it back.

My Lord ...

> "38 For I am persuaded, that neither death, nor life, nor angels, nor principalities, nor powers, nor things present, nor things to come, 39 Nor height, nor depth, nor any other creature, shall be able to separate us from the love of God, which is in Christ Jesus our Lord."
>
> Romans 8:38-39

Open your heart and invite God into every circumstance because when Good enters the scene, miracles happens!

My Lord ...

I love You Lord with all my heart and nothing I do can tear us apart.

You are a Man who can not lie, You promised to protect me until I die.

I seek You Lord each and every day, I pray and ask You Lord to teach me Thy way.

Thank You Lord for loving me,

I will praise You always because

You are worthy.

Fighting to Live

TO LIVE IS TO FIGHT……I AM A BREAST CANCER SURVIVOR, A LEUKEMIA WARRIOR, A FORMER ADDICT, A CONGESTED HEART FAILURE VICTOR.

> "Life has knocked me down a few times. It has shown me things that I never wanted to see. I have experienced SADNESS and FAILURES. But one thing is for sure, I ALWAYS GET BACK UP."
> - Author Unknown

Now this one is thorough and straight to the point. Anyone who has followed me on my Facebook social media page over the years knows the hell, trials, tribulations and toils I experienced.

I was inspired to write about what happened after reflecting back on what all God has brought me through, enabling me to claim the VICTORY in the end.

I had literally suppressed all the pain, hurt, disappointments, regret, helplessness, anger, frustration, shame, fear and doubtful memories of the whole situation.

God brought it back to my remembrance being that I still had some things He needed to remove. Until I allowed those memories and feelings to resurface, He could not finish the work He begun in me that needed to be completed.

GOD KEPT ME THROUGH IT ALL AND THAT IS WHY I WANTED TO PUBLISH MY POEMS. WHAT DOESN'T KILL YOU OR BREAK YOU MAKE YOU STRONGER RIGHT?

Everything I have been through had a significant and meaningful purpose in my life.

I probably would not be the STRONG woman I am today if God had not allowed me to go through them...

THANK YOU, FATHER GOD YAHAWA, GIVING YOU ALL THE PRAISE GLORY!

Fighting To Live

The year of 2016 was one of the most HUMBLING times of my LIFE, being diagnosed with Stage 3 Metastatic Estrogen Positive Breast Cancer....that wasn't my biggest fight.

On February 7, 2012 God delivered me from the stronghold addiction of CRACK COCAINE, and while going through CHEMOTHERAPHY treatments I faced it once again.

I was living with someone who at the time just couldn't break their habit, instead of being that STRONG MAN OF GOD he chose to become an ADDICT.

Holding TIGHTLY to my FAITH it became clear to me as I fought not 1 battle but 2, knowing God was with me through it ALL, that was a battle I WAS NOT DESTINED TO LOOSE.

In 2020 I am living with DEPRESSION and the STRUGGLE IS REAL you see, but when I am FIGHTING TO LIVE I call on God because He will once again SET ME FREE.

Amen

> "He giveth power to the faint; and to them that have no might he increaseth strength."
>
> Isaiah 40:29

Life has knocked me down quit a few times and many times I wanted to just give up.

God has a way of reminding me that my work here isn't finished, showing me why I should keep pressing through, and that I am never alone.

He has been there with me through all the heartaches, break downs, thoughts of killing myself, tribulations, hopelessness, lack of faith, weakness and every bad decision I ever made.

I can't praise Him enough for how far he has Brought me, all the victories we have won, and those we have yet to win.

Amen

Amen, Amen I praise Your name no matter what you're always the same.

I come to You before the throne for strength and endurance to carry on.

Lord, You Are Awesome!

Lord, You Are Great!

Lord, You Are worthy to be praised!

Catch It, Check It, Change It

The title to this poem stems from a class I attended for my mental imbalance health concerns after my Primary Care Physician referred me to the program upon my request due to going through a very stressful time at home.

As I was going on with my evening, everything was fine until I began having these sudden flashes of negative, judgmental thoughts taking over my mind.

I quickly accessed my thoughts by asking God to help me and to remove them. Knowing that God will hold me accountable for every word spoken or written and every thought that is dwelled upon or caused us to go against His will, I remembered the 3 C's.

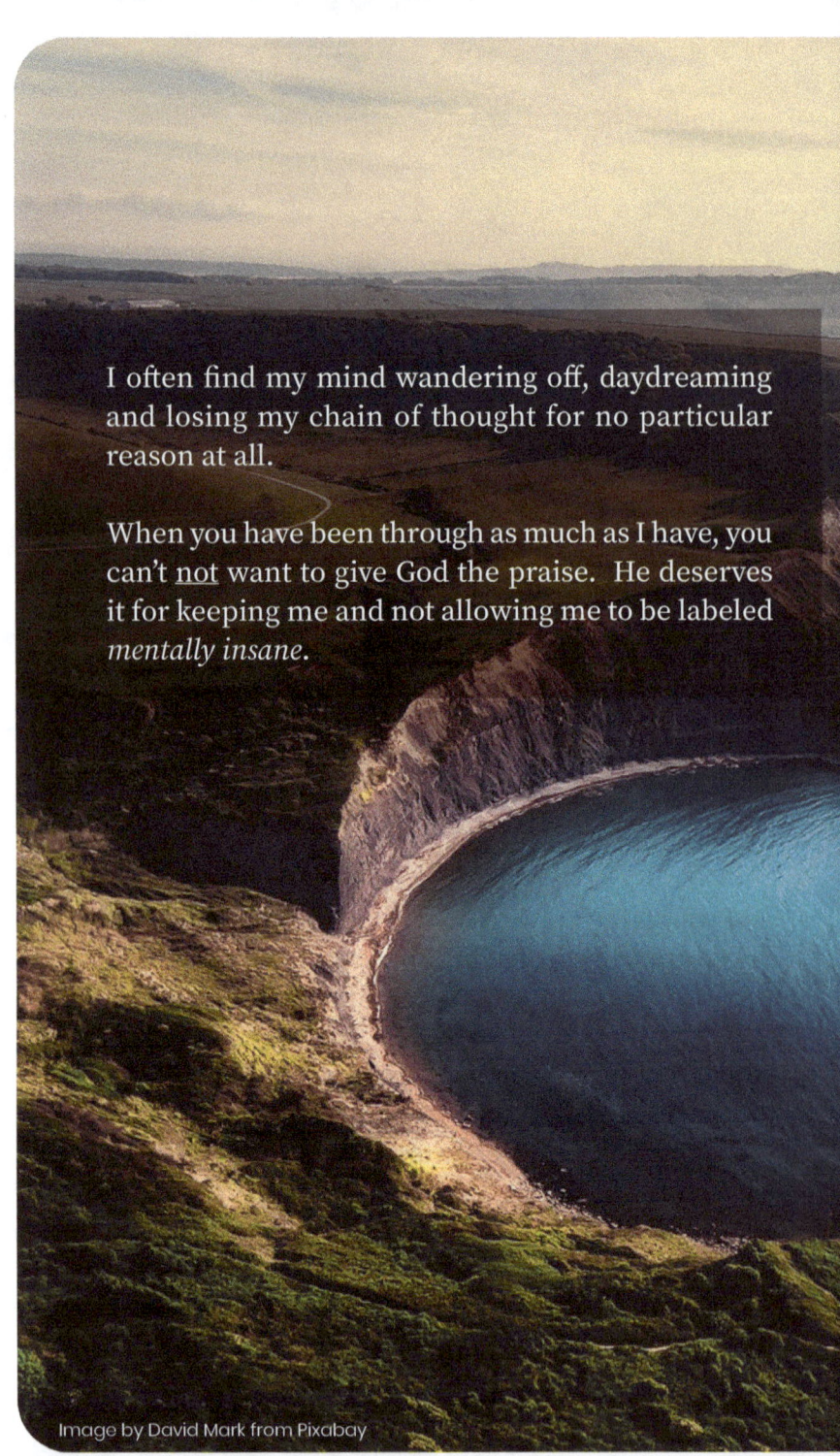

I often find my mind wandering off, daydreaming and losing my chain of thought for no particular reason at all.

When you have been through as much as I have, you can't <u>not</u> want to give God the praise. He deserves it for keeping me and not allowing me to be labeled *mentally insane*.

Catch It, Check It, Change It

Stop with the thoughts, are you trying to drive me insane? Then I begin to think of Yahawa's goodness and how He shelters me from the rain.

Lord I ask that You forgive me for all my daily sins I am confessing to You these things for today because tomorrow I will be repenting again.

Unsolicted Memories

This poem was written as I meditated on a page from one of my Daily Devotionals. You will read about reactions to my interactions with our #1 enemy Satan himself.

I have a sleep disorder called Narcolepsy, which causes the patient to have very vivid and terrified hallucinations upon waking from sleep.

I was misdiagnosed with PTSD which is what I am being treated for, and have not been re-accessed or treated for Narcolepsy as of yet.

The hallucinations for me started after taking medication for my mental imbalance that was prescribed by a mental health worker (I was not experiencing anything like this before taking this medication).

I requested to be taken off that particular medication due to the horrifying hallucinations I began to see, but the medication had already done its damage. They took me off of the medication immediately and years later I am still seeing hallucinations.

Everything I see appears as a black silhouette of a figure, with no other detailing features —just the outline shape of cats, spiders, walking 6-foot flowers, human shaped things, etc.

I am told by Cleo (my fiancé) that I curse worse than a sailor when I am dreaming, being that I don't do that when I am awake.

He has been kicked, scratched, bitten, punched, elbowed and kneed—which I never used to do those things before taking that medication.

Some of the incidents I can't remember or recall until I am made aware by him.

Every poem in this book gives you a glimpse of the victories I have won and the ones I am still fighting, and have yet to win the victory over.

Giving All Praises to the Most High For the Victories to Come

Unsolicited Memories

LEAVE ME ALONE SATAN, before I tell my
FATHER on you! Trying to trick me with your
lies, can't you see that it's God that I choose?!

Coming to in my dreams in the middle of the
night, reminding me of my sinful past NOW
YOU KNOW THAT AIN'T RIGHT!!

I SCREAM, I CUSS, I FIGHT & I SHOUT,
but when I wake up in the morning I can't
remember what it was all about.

Giving PRAISES to my Lord for the restoration
of my mind, it is because of the daily mercies
He gives that I am able to write these rhymes.

About the Author

Kimeisha D. Cox wrote her first poem in 2012 after being delivered from the stronghold of a drug addiction. Each poem has a significant meaning and tells a story of how she was able to overcome and when the VICTORY over every obstacle she faced which is the title of this book POETIC PRAISES was born.

She is the proud mother of 1 Son, A Daughter (in law) & 4 Beautiful Grandchildren.

She is also an Entrepreneur and the owner of 2 successful businesses: CROWNS OF GLORY FAMILY HAIR CARE & UNIQUELY DE'VINE CUSTOMS DESIGNS.

In her free time she loves listening to her gospel playlists, spending time with fiancé / business partner, family and her 2 fur babies Maxx And Reign.

This is the first book she has published but definitely not her last.

Acknowledgments

First and foremost I want to THANK MY FATHER IN HEAVEN for without Him none of this would be possible.

TO ALL my Alumni Sisters and Peers from the Atlanta Mission (Women & Children Shelter, Personal Development Program/ PDP) Counselors and Extended Staff Members for the support and encouragement you gave to me, which inspired me to write a book.

A SPECIAL THANKS goes to Ms. Maria for allowing me to be a part of the Atlanta Mission Community News Letter which enabled me to write my first Article for the column titled, "Am I My Sister's Keeper".

To Mr. Calvin, an Alumni Brother from the Atlanta Mission (Men's Program The Shepherd's Inn). He gave me an opportunity to write a personal heartfelt one of a kind poem for his sister and it was the first project that I received paid compensation for.

To My Son Michael, who ALWAYS believed in me no matter what road this journey called life took me and for his UNCONDITIONAL love.

To my Daughter (in law) Marshell "Shay" for putting up with me during the hardships I went through when I had nowhere else to go.

To my GRANDBABIES Michael "Trea, Grandma Pooh" the 3rd, Saniyah "Na-Na", Sherice "Re-Re", and Stephanie "Fe-Fe" for all the LOVE, LAUGHS and SPECIAL MOMENTS we shared together.

To Pastor Michael A. Shinn & Lady Eunice Shinn and my entire New World Harvest Baptist Church family for ALL the outstanding love and support you provided for me when I was diagnosed with

Stage 3 Metastatic Estrogen Positive Breast Cancer (2016).

To Pastor Arthur Carson & First Lady Carson for the STRENGTH you gave by growing my Faith and allowing me to be a Member of Springfield Baptist Church after God delivered me from the stronghold of a 20 year Crack addiction (2012).

To Cleven, My Love, My Better Half..... THANK YOU for loving me and always keeping me laughing. You keep me grounded by encouraging me to go for my dreams and STAND UP against all doubts by being the strong woman of God I was created to be.

To my family for LOVING me through ALL THE HEARTACHES I caused when I felt like I wasn't worthy of your love.

To Shawn (Solo-Xquizit) for the encouraging support you offered by letting me know how important it is to protect my written work by having it copywritten and sending me links to open poetry events.

I would also like Acknowledge & Thank Pastor Dr. R.K.Turner , his wife First Lady Lynnette Stanley Turner & The Mount Vernon Baptist Church Family in Atlanta Ga for allowing me to become a temporary member of their church family in the absence of not being able to attend my original home church also in Atlanta Ga Springfield Baptist Church where Pastor Arthur Carson Presides. I joined Springfield Baptist Church in March 2012 after God delivered me the stronghold of a drug addiction. I served as a faithful member joining the choir, attending Bible Study & Both Sunday Services until I became a resident at Atlanta Missions Women & Children (PDP) Program in October of 2012.

www.ingramcontent.com/pod-product-compliance
Lightning Source LLC
Chambersburg PA
CBHW061952070426
42450CB00007BA/1320